EARTH-FRIENDLY
WASTE
MANAGEMENT

CHARLOTTE WILCOX

LERNER PUBLICATIONS COMPANY · MINNEAPOLIS

The text of this book is printed on Lustro Offset Environmental paper, which is made with **30 percent recycled post-consumer waste fibers**. Using paper with post-consumer waste fibers helps to protect endangered forests, conserve mature trees, keep used paper out of landfills, save energy in the manufacturing process, and reduce greenhouse gas emissions. The remaining fiber comes from forestlands that are managed in a socially and environmentally responsible way, as certified by independent organizations. Also, the mills that manufactured this paper purchased certified renewable energy, such as solar or wind energy, to cover its production.

Lerner Publications Company
A division of Lerner Publishing Group, Inc.
241 First Avenue North
Minneapolis, MN 55401 U.S.A.

Website address: www.lernerbooks.com

Library of Congress Cataloging-in-Publication Data

Wilcox, Charlotte.
    Earth-friendly waste management / by Charlotte Wilcox.
       p.   cm. — (Saving our living Earth)
    Includes bibliographical references and index.
    ISBN 978-0-8225-7560-3 (lib. bdg. : alk. paper)
    1. Refuse and refuse disposal—Juvenile literature. 2. Recycling (Waste, etc.)—Juvenile literature. I. Title.
    TD792.W548 2009
    363.72'8—dc22   2008001883

Manufactured in the United States of America
2 3 4 5 6 7 — DP — 14 13 12 11 10 09

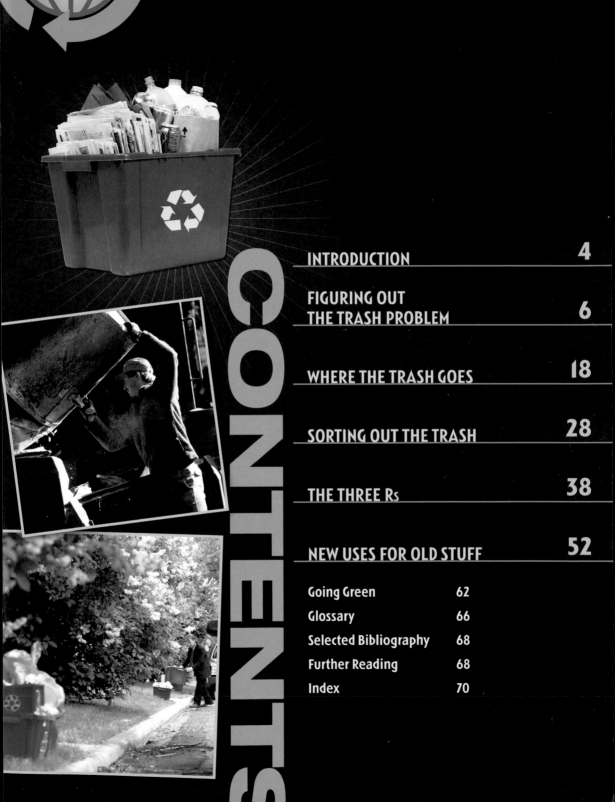

CONTENTS

INTRODUCTION

Imagine you are at the Kennedy Space Center. You are about to watch a space shuttle lift off. But instead of one launchpad, imagine thousands. Lined up, side by side, are 2,700 space shuttles. They stretch for 125 miles (200 kilometers). That is about as far as from New York City, New York,

A garbage truck dumps trash in a landfill. As the world's trash problem grows, people need to find workable solutions for dealing with all of the rubbish.

to Philadelphia, Pennsylvania. Then think about this: The weight of that many space shuttles equals the amount of trash people throw away worldwide in one day.

Trash piles up on Earth at 6 million tons (5.5 million metric tons) a day. That's more than 2 billion tons (1.8 billion metric tons) a year. What to do with all this rubbish is a huge problem. Some people suggest blasting it off to outer space. But it would take thousands of spaceships making trips every day to get rid of it. For now, rubbish must stay on Earth. And people must deal with it.

The business of handling trash is called waste management. The waste management system includes the people who collect, haul, sort, process, burn, and bury refuse. It includes the places where the trash ends up. The flow of refuse from its source through the waste management system is called the waste stream.

Too much waste is harmful to our health and the environment. Refuse contains germs, chemicals, and gases that can make people and animals sick. Unmanaged waste pollutes water, soil, and air.

Burying trash takes up thousands of acres of land. This land is needed for building houses and growing food. It takes lots of fuel to haul trash away. It takes additional fuel for bulldozers to bury it. Fuel is expensive, and burning fuel harms the environment.

Reducing waste saves money and resources for more important things. Less waste means less pollution. And reducing waste is something everyone can do.

CHAPTER ONE

FIGURING OUT THE TRASH PROBLEM

Where do 2 billion tons (1.8 billion metric tons) of trash come from each year? Most of it is everyday items that people throw away. It's the pizza you didn't finish last night. It's the carton it came in. It's your class notebook from last semester. It's the tennis shoes you wore out last summer.

People throw away more trash than in any previous century. We have disposable everything—from diapers to dishes to cameras. In the United States, each person throws away an average of 4.5 pounds (2 kilograms) of rubbish a day. This rate has stayed about the same since 1990. In 1980 each person threw away about 3.5 pounds (1.6 kg) per day. In 1960 it was about 2.5 pounds (1.1 kg) per day. Where to put all this unwanted stuff is a challenge.

WASTE AROUND THE WORLD

The United States throws away more trash than any other country. Here's a look at the amount of trash thrown away each day by people in countries throughout the world.

COUNTRY	POUNDS (KG) OF TRASH PER PERSON PER DAY
United States	4.5 (2)
Iceland	4.4 (2)
Netherlands	3.7 (1.7)
United Kingdom	3.5 (1.6)
France	3.2 (1.5)
Japan	2.5 (1.1)
Canada	2.1 (1)
Mexico	1.9 (.9)

Background image: Bags of garbage beside an apartment building await trash day.
Right: A display at the Centre for Alternative Technology in Wales illustrates how much trash an average family throws away in one year.

TRASH IN THE PAST

People in ancient times had trash, just as we do. They got rid of it in the same ways we do. They dumped it, burned it, or recycled it. The difference is that they didn't make as much of it.

Before the twentieth century, most people lived on farms. They reused and recycled almost everything. They sewed worn-out clothes into quilts. They fed food scraps to the chickens and pigs. They reused their containers. They recycled newspapers for toilet paper and insulation.

> Before the twentieth century, most people reused and recycled almost everything.

8

The things they did throw away were few in number. These were things like broken jars and worn iron pots. People buried or dumped them in remote places.

People in towns had more trash than their country neighbors. They bought more items, so they generated more waste from packaging. (But they also reused a lot of the packaging.) In town, people could not bury their trash. They burned what they could. The rest they often simply threw out into the street.

The problems grew worse as cities got bigger. Athens, Greece, had one of the world's first waste-management laws. No one could dump trash in or near the city. Athens started the first city dump in about 500 B.C.

CITY BLUES

By A.D. 1000, Europe had several large cities. London, England, and Paris, France, were among the largest. Houses stood close together along narrow, winding streets.

Ditches ran down the sides or center of the streets. People threw more than just solid waste into the streets. They threw wash water and sewage, or toilet waste, into the streets too. There it mixed with animal dung and other waste.

Rain washed the sewage into the ditches, which drained into rivers. Millions of rats, mice, and insects lived in the ditches. Wild dogs, cats, and pigs roamed city streets, eating garbage. In crowded areas, the smell of refuse filled the air.

Cities started to pass laws to clean up the streets. In 1280 London made it illegal to throw refuse in the streets. But this law failed to work. It provided no place for people to put their waste.

THE FIRE THAT CLEANED UP A CITY

In 1665 a great plague hit London. Rats and filth spread the sickness. About seventy thousand people—one in seven— died that year.

The next year another tragedy struck. A huge fire broke out in central London. It roared for four days before it burned out. The fire destroyed more

Firefighters in London fought fires that broke out throughout the city in 1666.

than thirteen thousand houses. It left two hundred thousand people homeless.

After the fire, fewer people got the plague. People believed the fire stopped the disease. But they didn't know why. Scientists at that time did not know about germs. They did not understand that germs spread diseases. They didn't know that germs grow very rapidly in garbage.

The fire helped the city in other ways. New streets were wider and straighter. The government provided better places for people to dump refuse. This helped keep the streets and rivers cleaner.

THE BEGINNINGS OF PUBLIC HEALTH

In 1842 an English government worker published a report. This report linked disease to dirty conditions in cities. The English government began efforts toward better waste management. They moved to keep refuse out of rivers. They worked to keep drinking water clean.

10

In the 1800s, London's crowded, unsanitary slums provided the perfect conditions for sicknesses to spread. By the mid-1800s, scientists began to link such unclean conditions to the spread of disease and worked to clean up cities.

This started the modern public sanitation movement. Public sanitation involves systems for getting rid of waste. It includes keeping water supplies clean and free of waste. In 1848 England passed the first Public Health Act. It required that every home have its own sanitation. This was usually a toilet or an ash pit. (People sometimes used ash pits in place of toilets. In an ash pit, human waste was covered with ashes to keep pests away and reduce odors.)

Doctors and scientists were just discovering the existence of germs. They learned that germs are what cause things to rot. They discovered that germs cause many diseases. These discoveries brought changes to cities in the United States and Europe.

Many cities began working on public sanitation. By 1870 many U.S. cities had organized trash collection. This was usually in the form of horse-drawn carts. They hauled the trash to a dump outside the city.

This horse-drawn cart was used for removing garbage in New York City.

Before specialized garbage trucks were made, early trash collectors used dump trucks, like the one at left from 1917.

In the early 1900s, trucks replaced horse-drawn carts. Early garbage trucks were simple dump trucks. The driver parked the truck in the street. He or a helper walked up to each house. They collected the trash and carried it to the truck.

A DIRTY JOB

Trash collectors' hands, hair, and clothes got horribly dirty. Filth, such as diaper refuse and rotten food, spilled on workers. Maggots fell from the garbage onto them. (These wormlike insects grow in decaying animal matter. They turn into flies when they mature.)

Sometimes workers got hurt. Rats in the trash occasionally bit them. Sharp glass and jagged tin cans cut them. Dangerous chemicals burned their skin.

OPEN DUMPS

When the truck was full, it went to a dump. The driver tipped the dump box and unloaded the trash. It fell out onto the ground and the truck drove away. Dumping trash came to be known as tipping.

This type of dump was called an open dump. It could be a field, riverbank, or hillside. Some dumps were large holes in the earth. In some places, workers periodically buried the trash. In other dumps, trash stayed on top of the ground.

Open dumps were dangerous places. They brought problems to people and animals. People sometimes came to open dumps searching for usable items. The germy garbage spread diseases to them. Wind blew trash around, sometimes toward nearby homes and towns. Wild animals came to open dumps to find food. Rats, snakes, and insects were everywhere. Birds flocked in to eat the insects and rotting garbage. Animals and birds got sick from drinking polluted water in open dumps.

This open dump located near a residential neighborhood in Pawtucket, Rhode Island, was photographed in 1912. Even though trash was being removed from city streets, open dumps did not solve many of the problems of waste and disease.

THE INDIANA JONES OF TRASH

William Rathje is an archaeologist who studies trash. He is a professor at the University of Arizona. Rathje and his students traveled to different locations to dig up trash. They found some surprises. One is that many foods do not decompose in landfills. Among the longest-lasting foods is the hot dog.

TROUBLE FOR THE ENVIRONMENT

Open dumps can seriously damage the environment. Chemicals in the trash run off into water and soil. They can harm plants and fish in lakes and streams. Fires often break out in old tires or dry trash. Poisonous smoke goes into the air.

As waste decays, it turns to liquid. It mixes with rainwater falling on the dump. This mixture, called leachate, is poisonous. It contains dangerous germs and chemicals. Leachate can make people and animals very sick. It is especially dangerous if it gets into water supplies.

Rainwater falling on an open dump soaks into the soil. The rain carries leachate with it deep into the ground. Here it reaches pockets of water called groundwater. Most well water comes from groundwater. If leachate gets into groundwater, it poisons nearby well water.

JEAN VINCENZ AND THE FRESNO LANDFILL

Public officials began to recognize these problems during the early 1900s. One pioneer of public sanitation was Jean Vincenz. He designed the first sanitary landfill. A landfill is a dump that buries trash every day. Vincenz's new landfill opened in 1937 in Fresno, California.

The Fresno landfill was a huge improvement over open dumps. Space was marked out for each day's rubbish. Trucks went to a selected spot to tip their

During its years of operation between 1937 and 1987, the Fresno, California, landfill received about 16,500 tons (14,970 metric tons) of waste each month.

trash. Bulldozers packed the trash down into trenches. Every day they covered all the trash with dirt. Then they packed everything down some more.

In 1941 the United States entered World War II (1939–1945). Vincenz left Fresno to join the U.S. Army Corps of Engineers. He built sanitary landfills at army posts. By 1944 more than one hundred army posts had sanitary landfills. Nearly one hundred U.S. cities also started using Vincenz's model.

A GROWING PROBLEM

The world changed in the years after World War II. People began to move away from farms. Millions moved to rapidly growing cities. Across the United States, cities became larger than ever. This shift in population meant more waste in less area.

At the same time, new product inventions appeared. Many of these products were disposable. More items came in their own packaging. People were throwing away more than they ever had. Trash piled up in city dumps like never before. Waste started to become a serious concern.

15

At a grocery store in New York in the 1960s, shoppers were able to recycle cans, glass, and plastic bottles.

16

REGULATING RUBBISH

As the solid waste problem grew, new laws were needed. Scientific discoveries showed new dangers of waste. The new laws tried to keep up with these discoveries. Congress passed the first national solid waste law in 1965. This law set goals for reducing and managing waste in Earth-friendly ways.

In the 1970s, Congress enacted laws to encourage recycling. They made open dumps illegal. They also made laws to regulate disposal of hazardous waste. Hazardous waste is especially dangerous to people and the environment.

In 1980 Congress set aside tax money in a special fund. The money is called the Superfund. It goes to clean up places that are highly polluted. The places the fund cleans up are called Superfund sites. Many Superfund sites were open dumps before 1979. They leaked leachate and other pollutants into the environment. So far the Superfund has cleaned up about 180 old dumps.

The United States continues to make progress in managing solid waste. We have national laws to encourage recycling oil from automobiles. Another law requires liners under landfills. The liners keep leachate from leaking out.

Since the 1980s, by law, all medical waste must be burned. Trucks and trains that haul waste must be sanitized before hauling food. Businesses that burn garbage must not pollute the air. Batteries must have labels to encourage proper disposal and recycling. Batteries cannot contain mercury. These laws help to keep waste pollution out of our air, water, and soil.

NOWHERE TO GO

A trash crisis occurred in 1987 on Long Island, New York. The landfills there were polluting groundwater. A businessman thought of shipping the rubbish south. He loaded a barge with several tons of rubbish.

The barge *(below)* launched on March 22. Three days later, it docked in North Carolina. But the governor wouldn't let it unload. It sailed to Louisiana, and then to Texas, and then to Florida. Nobody wanted it.

The barge sailed south to Cuba, and then Belize. Mexico threatened to shoot if it sailed there. After two months at sea, the barge returned to New York. There it docked for another three months. Finally officials decided to burn the rubbish in Brooklyn. They hauled the ashes back to landfills on Long Island. The trash ended up back where it had started.

CHAPTER TWO

WHERE THE TRASH GOES

Clean, modern trucks pick up most trash. These trucks have packers to pack down the trash. Trucks can haul more rubbish if it is packed. They can haul 4 to 10 tons (3.6 to 9 metric tons) of compacted waste. Smaller trucks pick up recyclable waste.

Some communities provide rubbish pick-up as a government service. People pay for the service with their taxes. In other areas, trash collection is a private business. People pay for it like they pay for phone service. Sometimes private businesses and the government cooperate to provide rubbish disposal.

A little over half of solid waste goes to landfills. About a third goes to recycling plants. These plants sort and process waste for reuse. Some waste goes to plants that use trash for fuel. Special kinds of waste go to special disposal facilities. These include medical waste, hazardous waste, and electronic waste, or e-waste.

PAY-AS-YOU-THROW

In most communities, people pay a set amount for rubbish pick-up. Pay-As-You-Throw is a new way to charge for rubbish service. People do not pay a set amount. Their payment is based on how much they throw away. The more trash, the higher the charge. This gives people a reason to reduce waste. The less they throw away, the lower their rubbish bill.

18

Background image: Modern trash collection involves trucks with compactors that enable trucks to haul more waste. *Left:* An aerial view of a landfill in Florida. *Below:* This plant in Peekskill, New York, burns garbage to make electricity.

NEW LANDFILLS

New landfills are getting harder to build. Many communities don't want them nearby. One of the biggest challenges is cost. A new landfill can cost $10 million to build.

Haulers pay to dump their trucks at disposal sites. This payment is called a tipping fee. Tipping fees help pay the costs of the disposal facilities.

There are about 1,650 landfills in the United States. In the 1970s, there were more than ten times as many. Most of those were open dumps, which were outlawed. Fewer landfills means they are farther apart. Many communities are 100 or more miles (160 or more km) from a landfill. That makes it costlier to get waste to the landfills

Ordinary garbage trucks are not designed for highway travel. They are designed for driving down neighborhood streets. So garbage trucks often take their trash to a transfer station. This is usually a nearby place where garbage trucks can easily travel.

Large semi trucks pick up trash from the transfer station. They haul it to a sanitary landfill farther away. An average semi trailer holds about 25 tons (22.7 metric tons) of waste. One semi can haul up to six loads from garbage trucks.

LAYERS OF THE LANDFILL

Modern sanitary landfills are much more than simple dumps. They are carefully engineered structures. They're designed to take up as little space as possible. Some landfills are designed so that the trash they hold gets piled up high. This helps reduce the space the landfills take up. But the sides of the landfill aboveground cannot be too steep. Steep sides could make the landfill crash. Each new level must be narrower than the level below. This makes some landfills look like giant, terraced pyramids.

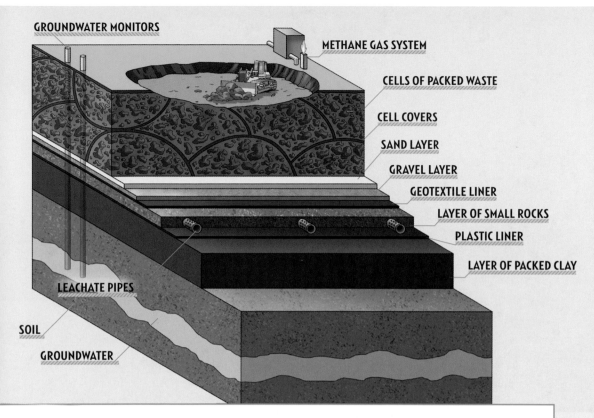

GROUNDWATER MONITORS

METHANE GAS SYSTEM

CELLS OF PACKED WASTE

CELL COVERS

SAND LAYER

GRAVEL LAYER

GEOTEXTILE LINER

LAYER OF SMALL ROCKS

PLASTIC LINER

LAYER OF PACKED CLAY

LEACHATE PIPES

SOIL

GROUNDWATER

In a sanitary landfill, layers of clay, rock, sand, and plastic keep leachate from entering the groundwater. Monitors also check groundwater for contamination. Blocks, or cells, of waste are covered with clay before more trash is added. Methane, an explosive gas that is produced when waste decomposes, escapes through vents and is burned off or can be used to produce electricity.

Landfills must control germs, pests, and odors. Earth, or fill, covers the trash to accomplish this. Landfills must hold lots of trash in a small area. This is done through a special method of packing, called compaction. Landfills must be engineered to keep leachate from leaking out. Layers of soil, rocks, and liners serve this purpose.

A sanitary landfill consists of several layers. The bottom layers are constructed before the landfill opens. The upper layers are constructed day by day as trash arrives. Usually builders dig a large hole first. They fill the bottom with packed clay. This is a heavy, dense type of soil. It forms a solid bottom for the landfill.

A layer of trash sits at the bottom of a newly opened sanitary landfill in California. The plastic liner can be seen on the hillside behind the trash.

Above the clay lies a huge sheet of heavy plastic. This liner covers the bottom and sides of the landfill. A layer of small rocks lies inside the plastic liner. The rocks keep waste off of leachate at the bottom. Some landfills have a second liner above this. The second liner is often a plastic fabric called geotextile. Its loose weave allows only liquids to pass through.

On top of the rocks and geotextile, builders add soil. Some landfills have more than one layer of soil. The lower layer is gravel, the top layer sand. The soil traps pieces of rubbish. It filters the leachate to make it all liquid at the bottom.

HOW THE SANITARY LANDFILL WORKS

Once the bottom layers are constructed, the landfill is ready to receive waste. Workers map out where each day's trash will go. Trucks drive into the landfill and dump their trash. Bulldozers pack it into a large block called a cell. Loaders dig dirt and cover the cell. Their giant wheels pack it down some more.

Compaction is very important in a landfill. If waste is not packed down enough, air pockets form. This can make the landfill unstable over time. Cave-ins and avalanches could occur. An avalanche happens when a large mass suddenly moves down the side of a hill.

Landfills use compactor equipment to pack the waste. Compactors are huge machines similar to bulldozers. Giant steel wheels with large teeth run over the trash. This cuts it up into small pieces.

SPACE-AGE DOZERS

Some landfills use high-tech gadgets in their heavy equipment. Compactors and bulldozers use Global Positioning System (GPS) units. These units bounce a signal to a satellite. The satellite beams back the exact location of the signal. This helps landfill workers measure the size of refuse cells. With GPS they can tell exact locations of each cell. They can tell exactly how well the cells are packed.

Compactors with special steel wheels made for grinding up trash move waste in this landfill.

Smaller pieces are easier to pack down. The compactor runs over the trash several times. Each run packs the trash a little tighter.

New cells are continually added, packed, and covered. Most landfills cover the trash every day. They use dirt or other cover materials. These include wood chips, foam, and products similar to sprayed-on concrete. Landfills that do not fill up a cell every day use temporary coverings. These are large blankets that cover the trash. They are made of plastic or geotextiles.

Beneath their covering of dirt, the cells begin to decay. This happens when bacteria and fungi eat the trash. These microscopic living things grow everywhere. Trillions of bacteria and fungi work to break down trash. They gradually turn some of the waste back into soil. Some items, such as soft foods, decay within days or weeks. Other materials, such as wood and leather, take years or decades. And still other things, such as glass, metal, and some plastics, do not decay at all.

The landfill layer system works with gravity to filter rotting waste. Solid pieces cannot pass through the many layers. Gravity pulls rainwater from the surface into the lower cells. Rainwater and rotten waste mix and turn to leachate. Gravity pulls the leachate down over time. Leachate begins to pool at the bottom of the landfill.

WORKING WITH LEACHATE

Raw trash is waste as it comes from the wastebasket or dumpster. It is bulky and made from many different materials. Leachate is easier to handle than raw trash. It can be made safe to return to the environment. But it needs to be treated before this can happen. The first step is to remove it from the landfill.

Leachate is collected through drains in the bottom of the landfill. Drain holes in the plastic liner connect to pipes. Leachate drains into the pipes deep beneath the surface. Pumps bring the leachate up to the surface.

Leachate, the liquid that separates from waste as it decomposes in a landfill, is pumped into a separate basin through a series of pipes.

Landfills treat leachate in a number of ways. One of the most common is with bacteria or fungi. The leachate is piped to tanks or ponds near the landfill. Here bacteria or fungi eat much of the harmful substances. This makes the leachate safe enough to spread on fields to fertilize farm crops.

LANDFILL GAS

As waste decays, it gives off natural gas. Landfill gas is about half carbon dioxide and half methane. These are greenhouse gases, which warm Earth's atmosphere. This contributes to global warming (the rising of Earth's temperature).

Methane burns very easily. In the past, the gas collected in pockets in landfills. Occasionally pockets near the surface would explode and burn. Modern landfills collect this gas and pipe it out. Many landfills burn the methane as it reaches the surface. The pipes come out of the ground and burn like torches. This gets rid of the gas but wastes a valuable resource.

Some landfills collect landfill gas for use as fuel. It can be used to generate electricity. It can fire furnaces and water heaters. It can power manufacturing plants. One million tons (907,185 metric tons) of waste create enough gas to generate one megawatt of electricity every day. That's enough to power seven hundred homes for one year.

WHEN A LANDFILL FAILS

Sanitary landfills are carefully designed and built. But sometimes they fail to contain trash properly. If trash is not covered quickly, it can blow around. Odors and pests soon appear. If trash is not packed down, areas can cave in or slide. If gas is not removed, fires can erupt. These problems are fairly easy to correct.

Burn stacks burn off methane at a landfill. Methane is produced when trash decomposes and can explode if allowed to pool.

TRASH AVALANCHE

In 2000 a tragedy occurred at a dump in the Philippines. Poor people in that country often search dumps for items to use or sell. On July 10, a huge mountain of rubbish caved in. The avalanche buried 205 people alive under filthy refuse. The landfill had to close for several months. As a result, the Philippine government passed laws for better waste management.

The worst failure of a landfill is leaking. If leachate gets into groundwater, it can present dangers to people. Chemicals in leachate may cause cancer. Lead and mercury can cause brain damage and other serious problems. Germs in leachate may spread diseases.

It is hard to determine when a landfill begins to leak leachate. The U.S. government requires most landfills to monitor nearby groundwater. Usually they drill wells in the area and test the water. These tests can determine if there is leachate in the water. If there is, an expensive cleanup must follow.

27

If leachate gets into groundwater, it can present dangers to people.

CHAPTER THREE

SORTING OUT THE TRASH

Scientists call everyday trash municipal solid waste. This is waste from homes, schools, and businesses. The trash is called municipal solid waste because often the municipality (city or town) takes care of it.

28

Municipal solid waste contains all kinds of stuff. It is about one-third paper. Much of it is packaging and containers. The rest includes leaves, food, clothing, plastic, metal, and glass. It also includes toys, furniture, dishes, appliances, and office supplies. Solid waste has some liquids in it. These are mostly from containers that are not empty.

Some kinds of solid waste are harder to dispose of. Large appliances are too bulky to go in a regular garbage truck. These include things like washing machines and kitchen stoves. Refrigerators and air conditioners have another problem. They contain chemicals that can harm the environment. Owners must haul appliances to special collection points for disposal.

Other types of solid waste need special handling too. These include e-waste, tires, and household hazardous waste. Only certain landfills can accept these types of waste.

Some items, like cell phones and household appliances, need special handling when they are disposed of.

This pie chart shows the amounts of different kinds of trash in municipal solid waste. The breakdown changes as people's needs and habits change.

30

E-WASTE

There are all kinds of electronic gadgets in use. New ones are being invented all the time. Many electronics last only a few months to a few years. This creates a lot of e-waste. Here are some examples of e-waste:

- Computers, monitors, and scanners
- Floppy disks and other electronic storage devices
- Printers and copy machines, plus the ink and toner cartridges they use
- Telephones, cell phones, and fax machines
- Televisions and radios
- Calculators, iPods, and handheld computers
- Cameras and camcorders
- Clocks, watches, and digital thermometers
- Electronic toys and games

- CDs, DVDs, videotapes, and machines that play them
- Tape recorders and tapes, phonographs and records
- Household electronics—coffeemakers, microwave ovens, and bread makers
- Small appliances like vacuum cleaners, toasters, irons, and sewing machines
- Electric tools such as drills and screwdrivers

People in North America toss out 136,000 computers every day. More than 100 million more computers already lie in landfills. So do about half a billion televisions, phones, and other electronics.

Although e-waste is mostly plastic, it also contains metal. A computer contains about thirty-five different kinds of metal. Some metals are dangerous if they get

Modern technology presents a unique set of problems in waste disposal, as new products quickly make old ones obsolete. Mercury, lead, and other materials in electronics become toxic in landfills.

Two-thirds of North American e-waste goes to other countries for recycling.

in water, soil, or air. The worst are mercury and lead. These can cause brain and kidney damage and other illnesses.

All these metals make e-waste dangerous to put in landfills. In nature these metals are always mixed with other types of rocks. After manufacturing the metals are much more concentrated. Bits of metal can get crushed in landfills. The metals might go into the leachate. They could get into water and soil.

Metals such as copper, gold, silver, and nickel in e-waste are valuable. But one computer or phone has only tiny amounts of metal. These metals have value only in larger amounts. They must be recovered from hundreds or thousands of machines. This takes many hours from many workers. That's why two-thirds of North American e-waste goes to other countries. There workers are cheaper to hire.

THE PROBLEM OF TIRES

In North America, we go through 300 million tires a year. We repair about 16 million of these. They go back on the road for a few more years. We recycle about 233 million. The rest go to landfills, get burned for fuel, or pile up.

Most landfills cannot accept whole tires. They cause too many problems. Tires take up lots of space and are hard to cut up. Their shape traps air underground. This makes the tires lighter than the earth around them. Over time the tires work their way to the surface. They pull decaying trash up with them.

Tires must be shredded before going in most landfills. A few special landfills can bury tires. These are monofills—landfills with only one kind of trash. The tires are buried in the monofill. They may still rise to the top. But they don't bring rotting trash up with them.

If tires don't get recycled, burned, or placed in a landfill, they pile up. All over the country, there are stockpiles of tires. Some of these stockpiles hold millions of tires. This is bad for the environment in several ways. For one thing, tires make good homes for mice, rats, and mosquitoes. These pests spread diseases.

Fire is also a danger with tire stockpiles. Burning tires release metals and oil into the ground and nearby water. The smoke contains smelly, poisonous gases. Tire fires are difficult and dangerous to put out. The only way to put them out is to cover the fire with dirt. Bulldozers must move the dirt, at great danger to the drivers. Tire fires sometimes burn for weeks or even months.

These shredded tires will be used as a drainage layer in a landfill near Canterbury, England. This landfill receives two hundred truckloads of waste a day.

HOUSEHOLD HAZARDOUS WASTE

Some household items are dangerous to include with regular trash. These are called household hazardous waste. They include things like cleaners, batteries, and insect sprays. Motor oil, antifreeze, and oil-based paint are also hazardous. These products may be safe to store on a shelf. But in the trash, containers easily break or spill. The contents could get into the environment. They could harm plants, animals, or people.

Americans toss 1.6 million tons (1.45 million metric tons) of household hazardous waste every year. Over three-fourths of hazardous waste in landfills is from homes. Some of these products occasionally hurt workers. Acid from car batteries will burn skin. Metal spray cans sometimes explode and cause cuts or eye injuries. Breathing fumes from dangerous chemicals can make workers sick.

Volunteers at a household hazardous waste collection site wear protective clothing and breathing masks.

Some people pour household hazardous waste down the drain or toilet. This practice is especially harmful to the environment. Household chemicals can poison water supplies. Pouring household hazardous waste down the drain contributes to pollution. It can pollute water in lakes and streams. This affects the health of plants, marine life, and people.

OTHER HAZARDOUS WASTES

Household hazardous waste and hazardous waste are not the same thing. Household hazardous waste consists of things we use in our homes. Hazardous waste comes from businesses and manufacturing plants. It consists of dangerous materials, often in large quantities.

Some hazardous waste is poisonous or gives off

DON'T FLUSH MEDICINES

People often flush leftover medicines down the toilet. This prevents other people or pets from getting into them. But flushing is dangerous because it lets harmful substances get in the water supply. Medicines also get in the water supply through human excrement.

In cities and towns, everything that is flushed down the toilet goes to a water treatment plant. In rural areas, it goes into a septic system. Either way the water is cleaned and eventually returns to lakes and streams. Water treatment removes germs and waste. But it is not as effective at removing traces of medicine. Medicines can harm animals and fish in lakes and streams. They harm people, too, when they get in drinking water.

Some community hazardous waste programs handle leftover medicines. People can drop off their unwanted medicines. Workers take them to a plant that burns them.

poisonous fumes. Some is hazardous because it might burn or explode. Some is corrosive. This means it can destroy or eat away materials that it touches. Laws regulate the production, use, transportation, and disposal of hazardous waste.

Special landfills can handle hazardous waste. These landfills take extra precautions to protect the environment. They are often built in places far from water sources. They usually have double liner systems to contain leachate.

Medical waste comes from hospitals, clinics, laboratories, and animal hospitals. It includes bandages, needles, gloves, masks, and surgical instruments. It includes removed body parts like tonsils or appendixes. Medical waste contains blood and germs that could spread disease. Doctors send these items to special medical waste disposal facilities. They burn wastes at high temperatures to kill all germs.

THE TIP OF THE ICEBERG

Municipal solid waste accounts for only two percent of all waste. The rest is industrial waste from manufacturing, farming, and mining. Industry, farms, and

Specially marked bags and boxes identify hazardous contents. Medical waste requires special disposal methods.

THINNER IS BETTER

When McDonald's made its drinking straws 20 percent thinner, the change caused less plastic to end up in the trash. The thinner straws eliminated 500 tons (454 metric tons) of solid waste in one year.

mines make far more waste than homes. Making 100 pounds (45 kg) of products can take 3,000 pounds (1,360 kg) of raw materials.

Industrial waste is cheaper to handle than municipal solid waste. Industrial waste is often produced as large piles of a single material. Ashes from burning coal at a power plant are one example. Mining dust or shells from a seafood factory are others. Usually the manufacturer pays for disposing of the waste. Individuals can help reduce industrial waste by buying fewer products.

Municipal solid waste is harder to take care of. One reason is that it comes in smaller quantities. It comes from many, many more places. Municipal solid waste contains a wide range of materials. These must be sorted before disposal or reuse. But everyone can help reduce municipal solid waste.

CHAPTER FOUR

THE THREE Rs

Landfills are the most common way of dealing with trash. But they are not the best way. Governments and waste management companies are working together on alternatives. They have created a plan called the waste management hierarchy. A hierarchy is a series of things listed in order of importance or preference.

The waste management hierarchy lists ways to handle trash. It starts with the best way. This is to throw away less to begin with. Next is to recycle as much as possible. Third is burning trash for fuel. The hierarchy ends with the least desirable, which is landfilling.

Reducing should be the biggest activity and landfilling the smallest. But right now it is the other way around. Over half of solid waste goes to landfills. Only about one-third gets recycled.

Far too much solid waste is ending up in landfills. People can help to solve this problem by doing three things: reducing, reusing, and recycling. These are known as the three Rs of waste management.

Facing page: Participants in an Earthworks-sponsored Recycle My Cell Phone campaign in Washington, D.C. Earthworks works with communities to protect the environment. *Below:* A waste treatment facility in Wijster, Netherlands, turns much of its trash into compost. The compost, which enriches soil, is sold for farm and garden use.

REDUCE WASTE

RECYCLE

BURN FOR ENERGY

LANDFILL

40

The methods for handling trash ranked from the most preferred at the top down to the least preferred at the bottom

REDUCING WASTE

Waste prevention is at the top of the waste hierarchy. It's a better option than reusing and recycling because it keeps waste from happening in the first place. Reducing waste takes no fuel, processing, land, or workers. All it takes is people who will do it. When we prevent waste, we keep landfills smaller. We also reduce the need for building more recycling plants.

Reducing waste starts with manufacturing. Many companies are working to make their products less wasteful. Companies are finding they can save money by reducing waste.

Lighter containers go a long way toward reducing waste. In 1977 a 2-liter (2.1 quarts) plastic drink bottle weighed 2.4 ounces (68 grams). The same bottle now weighs about 1.8 ounces (51 g). This keeps 250 million pounds of plastic out of the waste stream every year.

REUSING THINGS

Reusing items keeps them from entering the waste stream. Anything that can be used over again saves landfill space. Reused items keep their original form.

PAPER OR PLASTIC?

We often hear this question at the supermarket. Paper and plastic bags are equally recyclable. But it takes 20 to 40 percent less energy to make a plastic shopping bag than a paper one. And plastic bags are much lighter and thinner than paper ones. It takes seven trucks to haul the same number of paper bags as one truckload of plastic bags. A better choice than paper or plastic is to bring your own reusable shopping bag.

Bring your own reusable shopping bags to the store to save on paper or plastic.

This is different from recycling, where items are broken down to create new products. Reuse is better than recycling because reused items need no processing or remanufacturing.

Many household items can be reused. Clean, empty food jars are good for storing leftovers. Used boxes make good storage bins. Books, magazines, and catalogs can go to libraries, hospitals, and nursing homes. Newspapers make great wrapping for gifts. Good used clothing, toys, and games can go to thrift stores. Worn-out clothing can become cleaning rags or pet bedding. You can

One artist made good use of old plastic bottles and cans by using them to make a scarecrow.

be creative and look for other ways to reuse rather than throw away.

Consumers can encourage companies to design better products. Replaceable parts make products last longer. If a new part will fix the item, you won't need to throw it away. Buying items with replaceable parts sends a message to manufacturers. It tells them people want to buy reusable products.

RECYCLING

The United States does better than most countries in recycling. Of the 4.5 pounds (2 kg) of rubbish each person tosses each day, about 1.5 pounds (0.7 kg) gets recycled. That's a recycle rate of about one-third of all trash. Different items are recycled at different rates. In the United States, people recycle:

- Ninety percent of newspapers and half of all papers
- Over two-thirds of corrugated boxes
- Two-thirds of steel
- Over half of all yard trimmings
- Half of all aluminum
- One-third of plastic bottles
- One-fourth of glass jars

Recycling saves resources. Recycling five thousand sheets of paper saves almost 200 gallons (750 liters) of water. It also saves 10 gallons (40 liters) of oil. Recycled aluminum uses only 5 percent of the energy needed to produce new aluminum.

Among the most-recycled items are lead-acid batteries. These batteries start cars, trucks, buses, boats, and train engines. They power golf carts, wheelchairs, campers, and electric cars. The United States recycles about 99 percent of its lead-acid batteries. Any place that sells new batteries will recycle old ones.

Most any type of metal, aluminum, paper, and plastic is recyclable. When it comes to glass, only bottles and jars are recyclable. Light bulbs, mirrors, windows, and dishes are made with different materials. These cannot be recycled (but we don't throw them away as often as we do bottles and jars).

43

A woman sorts recyclables at this recycling center in Morris Plains, New Jersey.

THE UNIVERSAL RECYCLING SYMBOL

People all over the world recognize the Universal Recycling Symbol. In 1970 a cardboard-recycling company sponsored an art contest. The contest was connected with the first Earth Day. Gary Anderson, a college student, created this design to enter in the contest. Judges chose Anderson's design from over five hundred entries. He won $2,500.

THE RECYCLING LOOP

Recycling is a loop, or circular process. This means that items end up where they started. Recycled items start out in homes, schools, and businesses. People use items and then collect what remains, such as leftovers and containers. After processing, these materials return to homes, schools, and businesses as new products. There are five steps in the recycling loop.

Step 1—Collection. People collect recyclable materials at homes, schools, and businesses. The most commonly recycled items are paper, cardboard, aluminum and metal cans, plastic bottles, and glass jars. Rubbish haulers or recyclers may pick up the items. Or people may drop them off at collection centers. Some recyclers pay for recycled items.

Larger recyclables need special handling. This includes things like tires, batteries, and steel from vehicles and appliances. They go to special recycling facilities that handle these materials.

Step 2—Processing. Recyclable trash goes to a recycling center, or materials recovery facility. This is a plant that sorts and processes waste for remanufacturing. Everything gets washed and dried. Then it is separated by type.

Metal is easy to separate with large magnets. Aluminum and paper each go on separate paths. Different types of plastic are separated by machine or by hand.

At the Sacramento Recycling and Transfer Station in California, workers sort out plastic, glass, paper, and aluminum cans for recycling.

Glass must be separated by color—clear, green, or amber (brown). This is because color cannot be removed once it's added to glass.

Some materials undergo more processing. Paper, glass, and plastics are chopped into small pieces. Each type of material is crushed and pressed into bales, or tightly bound bundles. Metals are melted and then hardened into blocks called ingots.

Step 3—Sale. Manufacturers buy bales or ingots of prepared materials. These are usually priced by weight. Prices go up or down depending on supply and demand.

Step 4—Manufacturing. Manufacturers use the materials to make new products. Some recycled materials turn into more of the same thing. Aluminum cans make new cans. Old, used paper makes new, recycled paper. Some recycled plastic becomes new plastic items such as bottles and bags. Other plastics turn

TREES FOR PAPER

Forty-two notebooks made of recycled paper save one tree from being cut down. One ton of recycled paper saves seventeen trees. But that is only part of the picture. Nearly all trees used for paper in the United States are specially grown for papermaking. These are young trees that were planted in special paper forests. Paper companies plant and harvest trees like any crop. For every tree they cut down, they plant a new one in its place.

This type of tree harvesting is good for the environment. Young trees give off more oxygen than old trees. Young trees also absorb more carbon dioxide than old ones. Keeping forests young and healthy promotes better air quality.

into clothing, camping gear, or building materials.

Step 5—Reuse. People buy goods made from recycled materials, completing the loop. Steel, aluminum, and glass can go around the loop forever. Paper and plastic can go around a limited number of times. The materials tend to break down after repeated processing. For that reason, recycled paper is usually a half-and-half mixture of new and recycled.

PLASTIC RECYCLING CODES

Most plastic containers have a number imprinted on the bottom. It usually appears inside the recycling symbol. Each number tells what type of plastic the container is made of. Many recycling centers recycle only plastic with numbers 1 and 2. Many stores recycle plastic coded with number 4. Special recyclers accept the other numbers.

Polyethylene terephthalate (PET or PETE). This is used mostly for drink bottles and mouthwash bottles. It recycles into new bottles, plastic jars, fabrics, carpet, and other products.

High-Density Polyethylene (HDPE). Milk, water, and juice jugs are made of HDPE. So are soap bottles, yogurt and margarine tubs, and trash and shopping bags. Recycled HDPE is made into new bottles, bags, building materials, and bulletproof vests.

Polyvinyl Chloride (PVC or vinyl). Rigid PVC is used for packaging, cooking-oil bottles, and building materials. Bendable vinyl is for film, bags, fake leather, and other items. It recycles into the same kinds of items. It also becomes flooring, traffic cones, and hoses.

Low-Density Polyethylene (LDPE). This plastic remains strong when pressed thin. It is good for shopping and food bags and squeezable bottles. LDPE recycles into shipping envelopes, trash bags, film, furniture, and building materials.

Polypropylene (PP). This is in ketchup and medicine bottles, reusable containers, yogurt and

---

THE BIG PICTURE

The camera you use makes a difference to the environment. Cameras that use film create hundreds of tons of solid waste each year. Photo processors can recycle disposable cameras. But not all do. No one keeps track of how many of these cameras go into landfills. Digital cameras create less waste. They use no film and no chemical processing.

margarine tubs, drinking straws, and diapers. Recycled polypropylene is made into auto parts, signal lights, brooms, bicycle racks, and other items.

Polystyrene (PS). The rigid-form plastic appears in medicine bottles and plastic tableware. It recycles into many household and office items. The foamy form, called Styrofoam, is used for hot-drink cups, egg cartons, and meat trays. It recycles as these same items. It can also be turned into insulation and foam packaging.

Other. This includes other types of plastic or a combination of plastics. Large water, juice, and ketchup bottles sometimes carry this imprint. These plastics recycle as bottles or plastic lumber.

COMPOSTING

One-fourth of all trash in U.S. landfills is food scraps and yard waste. Another one-third is paper and cardboard. Composting could keep these materials out of landfills.

Compost is a mixture of rotting plant and animal material. This may include leaves, grass, food, paper, manure, and certain other wastes. Compostable materials are mixed together in an outdoor pile or bin. With the right amount of moisture and air, bacteria begin to grow. This causes the pile to decay. As the decaying process continues, fungi and insects join the pile.

GRASSCYCLING

A simple way to reuse lawn clippings is grasscycling. This means leaving grass clippings on the lawn. Grasscycling provides natural fertilizer for the lawn. It saves landfill space and doesn't cost a cent.

Kitchen scraps *(left)* turn into rich compost *(right)* that can be used to add nutrients back into the soil for growing gardens and crops.

Bacteria, fungi, and insects break down the material into small particles. Over time, they turn the compost into dark, rich soil. This takes several months to a year or two. Compost makes excellent fertilizer for lawns, trees, gardens, and houseplants. It keeps plant and animal wastes out of landfills.

Backyard composting requires instructions and some easy-to-make equipment. There are also larger, community-based compost piles. People bring compostable materials to the pile. When the compost becomes fertilizer, they can take some home.

BURNING TRASH FOR FUEL

The United States burns about 33 million tons (30 million metric tons) of trash for fuel each year. This helps keep trash out of landfills. It also helps reduce the need for coal, oil, and natural gas. These fuels pollute the environment.

Waste must be treated before it can become fuel. First, workers must sort it out. They must remove everything made of metal or glass. Tires must come out too. About 80 percent of the waste is left. It contains paper, food, leaves, grass, plastic, wood, and other materials.

Machines shred the trash into small pieces. It is dried and pressed into pellets,

A worker at a landfill in Michigan adjusts settings on a methane gas recovery system. The methane is collected from decaying garbage in the landfill and then used to generate electricity for customers of a Michigan-based energy company.

bricks, or logs. This makes it easier to handle. The result is called refuse-derived fuel.

Refuse-derived fuel often takes the place of coal. It takes 4 pounds (2 kg) of waste to replace 1 pound (.4 kg) of coal. Electric companies buy refuse-derived fuel to power their generators. Some governments and businesses buy it to heat large buildings.

FLYING RECYCLABLES

People in the United States throw away enough aluminum in three months to rebuild every commercial airplane in the country.

There are about ninety refuse-derived fuel plants in the United States. Worldwide there are about six hundred plants in thirty-five countries. The United States burns about one-seventh of its trash for fuel. Denmark, Switzerland, and France burn about half of theirs.

51

CHAPTER FIVE

NEW USES FOR OLD STUFF

People and families have recycled things for thousands of years. Papermakers have used recycled materials for several hundred years. Large-scale recycling by manufacturers is about one hundred years old. Some of the most common items made with recycled materials include aluminum cans, carpeting, cereal boxes, comic books, egg cartons, glass containers, laundry detergent bottles, nails, newspapers, paper towels, steel products, and trash bags.

The future is looking brighter for recycled products.

52

Up until the twenty-first century, many products cost more to recycle than to make. Recycled paper, for example, was more expensive than new paper. Recycled plastic was also more expensive. That is changing. Manufacturers are finding many new ways to use recyclables. They are learning that recycling can save money. The future is looking brighter for recycled products.

PLASTIC LUMBER

Recycled plastic makes good lumber. Boards made of recycled plastic don't need to be painted. This makes plastic lumber popular for decks and fences.

Background image: Designed by staff and students from Oatridge College in Scotland, the first-prize-winning display at the 2007 Gardening Scotland show featured old tires, aluminum cans, recycled boots, and a greenhouse made of empty bottles. *Below:* Visitors at Yellowstone National Park's Old Faithful sit on benches made from recycled plastic.

This boardwalk at the Fradley Pool Nature Reserve near Litchfield, England, is made of recycled plastic boards.

Wood lumber must be treated with chemicals to make it last longer. These chemicals can harm the environment. Plastic lumber does not need these treatments. It can last more than three times longer than wood. Insects don't eat plastic like they do wood, either.

Wood rots if it sits in water, but plastic does not. This makes plastic lumber good for docks, boardwalks, and bridges. A plastic lumber bridge at Fort Leonard Wood, Missouri, was built in 1998. It used 6.5 tons (5.8 metric tons) of recycled plastic. That's equal to 78,000 milk jugs and 335,000 Styrofoam cups.

One problem with plastic lumber is that it can sag in heat. Recycling companies are working on ways to prevent sagging. This improvement would encourage more builders to use plastic lumber.

FABRICS FROM PLASTIC

Polyester cloth is made of the same material as plastic drink bottles. That makes it easy to recycle these bottles into fabrics. Just five plastic soda bottles make one extra-large T-shirt or one ski-jacket filler. Twenty-seven bottles make a sweater, and thirty-five bottles make a sleeping bag. Any fabric containing polyester might be partly recycled.

Nonwoven fabrics are also made from recycled plastic. These fabrics begin as sheets of melted, recycled plastic. The plastic cools into a soft, strong fabric. Nonwoven fiber looks something like paper. It is impossible to tear but easy to cut with scissors. It is waterproof, lightweight, and makes comfortable clothing.

Some workers wear nonwoven clothing over their regular clothes. Nonwoven fiber is made into lab coats, coveralls, and even full body suits with hoods. These protect workers' clothing from things like oil and paint.

A worker checking on chemical storage drums wears a protective Tyvek suit made from nonwoven fabric.

Camping gear, such as this tent, is often made from nonwoven fabric. The fabric is lightweight, strong, and waterproof.

The strength of nonwoven fibers makes them good for shipping envelopes and building materials. It's good for camping gear because it's waterproof. Some countries print money on nonwoven fabric. It works well because it does not wear out. Nonwoven fiber can be recycled several times.

GAS FROM TRASH

Petroleum, also called crude oil, is one of the most valuable products on Earth. It's so valuable that it's called black gold. One barrel, or 42 gallons (159 liters), of crude oil produces more than 44 gallons (166 liters) of petroleum products. (This is because some of the oil expands during refining.) Crude oil is made into gasoline, diesel fuel, jet fuel, and heating fuels. It is also an ingredient in plastic, soap, ink, crayons, deodorant, and bubble gum.

The United States is the third-largest producer of crude oil in the world. However, Americans use 20 million barrels of oil every day. For this reason, the United States buys more than half of its oil from other countries. These countries control the price Americans pay for oil.

What if we could turn something worthless into black gold? That is what some companies are trying to do with waste. There are several different methods for turning trash into oil. Most of these have not been tried on a commercial scale.

One method being used at a plant in Missouri since 2004 appears to be successful. The plant takes garbage from a turkey-processing plant and grinds it up in machines. The machines break the feathers, bones, and other unwanted turkey parts into tiny pieces. The plant also adds water to the mixture. Next, the mixture flows through a series of tanks. The tanks heat it to 500°F (260°C), put

These glass vials (bottles) contain different grades of fuel oil made from leftover turkey parts.

57

POOP POWER

Some farms are beginning to turn animal manure into energy. There are two ways to do this. One is to burn the manure to produce electricity. The other is to let the manure rot, which creates natural gas.

England has the largest manure-burning plant in the world. It burns about 463,000 tons (420,000 metric tons) of chicken and turkey manure in a year. That amount produces enough electricity to power a small city.

it under pressure, then cool it. This turns the turkey parts into oil. The process takes about two hours. It can turn 1 ton (0.9 metric ton) of turkey parts into 600 pounds (272.2 kg) of oil. The oil can then be refined to make gasoline.

Japan and the United Kingdom recycle plastic into gasoline. These countries have special plants that can take any type of plastic. The plastic does not have to be washed or sorted. Machines grind the plastic and heat it under pressure. The machines produce about 5,000 gallons (19,000 liters) of fuel a day. The fuel works in any engine that can burn manmade fuel.

A different type of waste-to-fuel plant is called a digester. This technology uses bacteria to turn refuse into gas. Waste is placed in a tank with water. Bacteria in

Turkey droppings *(shown left)* can be used as fuel to make electricity. A power plant in Minnesota burns more than 500,000 tons (454,000 metric tons) of poultry litter per year.

the water break the waste down into a substance that can be used for fuel.

A highly efficient digester was developed in 2006 at the University of California. It separates bacteria into two different tanks. It works more quickly than older types of digesters. The new digester can turn 3 tons (2.7 metric tons) of food scraps into enough energy to power twenty-five homes for a day!

CHALLENGES TO EARTH-FRIENDLY WASTE MANAGEMENT

North America has come a long way in the quest to improve its waste management systems. But there is still a long way to go. Some items that could be recycled are not. One example is packaging peanuts. These small bits of foamy plastic are easy to recycle. But it costs too much to collect them. Because they are so lightweight, it takes mountains of them to make other products. Consequently, the cost of recycling the peanuts outweighs the value.

This equipment at a waste disposal plant uses bacteria to break down waste disposal sludge. Methane produced by the process can be turned into energy.

Cost is a challenge when it comes to recycling any type of product. Recycling is very expensive. It costs $50 to collect, haul, sort, and process a ton of recyclables. The average selling price for those recyclables is thirty dollars. Governments sometimes help pay for recycling to make up the difference. But recycling is still not very cost effective.

Another problem with recycling is that some people don't want recycling plants in their communities. The plants can be noisy. Many trucks may drive in and out of the plants every day. When people object to plans for a new recycling center near their homes, they exemplify an attitude known as NIMBY, or **n**ot **i**n **m**y **b**ackyard. This attitude makes it hard to build new recycling centers.

People need to be educated about the value of recycling. We also need

60

RECYCLING FOR FREEDOM

One of the biggest recycling projects ever was completed in 2008. The United States Navy built a ship out of steel from the World Trade Center. This building in New York City was attacked by terrorists on September 11, 2001. The attack brought the twin towers of the skyscraper down. They became two giant heaps of twisted, crumpled steel.

Twenty-four tons (22 metric tons) of this steel were melted down to become part of the USS *New York (below).* This new ship is as long as a city block. It cost one billion dollars to build. It will carry more than one thousand sailors and marines. The motto of the USS *New York* is "Strength forged through sacrifice. Never forget."

to keep finding new ways to reduce waste. Scientists are looking for more ways to turn trash into usable products. In the meantime, all of us can constantly look for ways to reduce, reuse, and recycle.

THE FUTURE OF WASTE MANAGEMENT

The waste hierarchy sets the goals for waste management. These are to throw away less, recycle more, turn trash into energy, and reduce landfilling. The three Rs show us how to reach those goals. Reducing, reusing, and recycling will result in less waste.

Energy recovery is the biggest frontier in waste management. Energy is one of the world's greatest needs. Everyone needs energy for transportation, heat, cooking, and electricity. And everyone has waste to get rid of. Turning waste into energy makes sense.

Students of today will be the scientists, educators, and public officials of tomorrow. Perhaps a reader of this book will pioneer new ways to turn waste into something useful.

WASTE-FREE LUNCH DAY

Mechanicsburg Middle School in Mechanicsburg, Pennsylvania, normally collects thirteen to fifteen bags of waste after lunch. In 2007 they held a waste-free lunch day. Students brought lunches in reusable lunch bags. Food was served in reusable containers and recyclable bottles. After lunch that day, the school collected just one bag of trash, one bag of recyclables, and half a bag of food waste.

GOING GREEN

Kids can help in the effort to reduce, reuse, and recycle. Here are a few ideas for you and your friends to try:

- **Shop green.** Before buying something, consider how you'll dispose of its packaging. Find out if the container is recyclable. Concentrated products, like frozen juice, save packaging. So do products that do more than one thing. An example is shampoo that includes conditioner. Better yet, look for items with no packaging. When possible, buy products made in your own community. Products made far away use huge amounts of fuel to get to you. Green shopping also means not buying things you don't need.

- **Throw away less.** Use things that are durable, or that last. Examples are reusable food containers and cloth shopping bags. Rechargeable batteries and refillable pens can be used many times. Use every bit of a product before tossing it. Give the toothpaste tube an extra squeeze. Add a little water to the shampoo bottle to get the last drop. Donate items you don't want instead of throwing them in the trash.

- **Pack a waste-free lunch.** An average school lunchbox is full of disposable packaging. The packaging from just one year's worth of lunches could generate as many as 67 pounds (30 kg) of waste. That adds up to 870 pounds (395 kg) of waste between kindergarten and twelfth grade! Packing lunches in reusable containers eliminates this waste.

A student at the Friends School of Minnesota empties lunch scraps into a compost pile. Composting keeps food waste out of landfills.

- **Eat all of your lunch.** Don't take more than what you know you'll eat. Food that does not get served can be donated to the hungry. But food left on your plate probably goes to a landfill.

- **Encourage your school to compost.** Schools can compost cafeteria waste. Compost makes good fertilizer for lawns, trees, and plants on school grounds and nearby parks. This saves the school money and keeps food out of landfills.

GOING GREEN

Tell government leaders your ideas about reducing, reusing, and recycling. Start with your school board. Other local leaders include members of your municipal, county, or parish government. These are people in your own community. They may help you put your ideas to work. You can also write to your state legislators and congressperson. Here are some tips:

- **Choose one idea or concern to write about.** Do you want to encourage your school to compost? Or would you like your city to open a recycling center for household hazardous waste? Zeroing in on one issue of importance to you will help bring focus to your letter.

- **Focus on the area served by the person you are addressing.** For example, don't write to your congressman about an idea for your school. That should go to your school board. And don't write to your mayor about a waste site in another part of your state. That should go to your state legislator.

- **Explain how your idea would help.** Give a short explanation of your idea. Then state why you think it would work. Tell about other schools or communities that have similar programs.

- **Be courteous.** This is important if you want leaders to seriously consider your idea. You must be respectful and positive. Offer your services to help carry out your idea. If someone responds, follow up with a thank-you letter.

ENVIRONMENTAL GROUPS

Many groups offer information about reducing and recycling. Here are just a few:

- **The Green Flag Program**
  http://www.greenflagschools.org
  Center for Health, Environment and Justice
  P.O. Box 6806
  Falls Church, VA 22040-6806
  703-237-2249

- **Healthy Child Healthy World**
  http://www.healthychild.org
  12300 Wilshire Boulevard, Suite 320
  Los Angeles, CA 90025
  310-820-2030

- **GrassRoots Recycling Network**
  http://www.grrn.org
  P.O. Box 282
  Cotato, CA 94931
  707-321-7883

GLOSSARY

aluminum: a lightweight, silver-colored metal often used for drink cans

avalanche: the sudden movement of a large mass, usually snow, down the side of a hill or mountain

bacteria: microscopic living things that exist everywhere on Earth. Some bacteria cause diseases, while many others are useful.

compost: a mixture of rotted plant and animal material used for fertilizer

geotextile: plastic fabric that can be used to line landfills

global warming: the warming of Earth because of increased carbon dioxide and other heat-trapping gases in the atmosphere. The theory of global warming has been supported by most scientific studies.

greenhouse gas: a name for carbon dioxide and other gases that hold the sun's heat near Earth. Greenhouse gases cause global warming.

groundwater: water that lies under Earth's surface

hazardous waste: dangerous waste materials that need special handling in order to be safely thrown away

household hazardous waste: leftover household products that are harmful to the environment when thrown away

industrial waste: waste from manufacturing, farming, and mining

landfill: a dump that buries trash

leachate: liquid that forms when decaying waste mixes with rainwater in a landfill

materials recovery facility: a plant that sorts and processes waste for remanufacturing. A materials recovery facility is the same as a recycling center.

medical waste: trash that comes from hospitals, clinics, laboratories, and animal hospitals. Medical waste often contains blood and other disease-causing materials.

mercury: a silver-colored, liquid metal that is poisonous

monofill: a landfill that accepts only one kind of trash

municipal solid waste: everyday trash that comes from homes, schools, and businesses

open dump: a place where solid waste is dumped and left uncovered

raw material: an unprocessed substance used to manufacture products

recycle: to process used or unwanted items so they can be used to make new products

recycling center: a plant that sorts and processes waste for remanufacturing. A recycling center is the same as a materials recovery facility.

refuse-derived fuel: fuel made from solid waste

sanitation: systems for cleaning water supplies and disposing of waste

sewage: toilet waste

waste management: the industry of collecting, handling, and disposing of wastes

waste stream: the flow of refuse from its source through the waste management system

SELECTED BIBLIOGRAPHY

Fletcher, Susan R., ed. *Summaries of Major Statutes Administered by the Environmental Protection Agency.* Washington, D.C.: U.S. Environmental Protection Agency, 2007.

Hickman, H. Lanier, Jr., and Richard W. Eldredge. "A Brief History of Solid Waste Management in the U.S., 1950–2000." *MSW Management,* Vol. 10, No. 5 (September/October 2000).

Merrill, Lynn. "Latitude, Longitude and Landfills." *Waste Age,* September 2007.

Miller, Chaz. "The Garbage Barge." *Waste Age,* February 2007.

Municipal Solid Waste in the United States: 2005 Facts and Figures. Washington, D.C.: U.S. Environmental Protection Agency, 2006.

Rathje, William L., and Cullen Murphy. *Rubbish! The Archaeology of Garbage.* Tucson: University of Arizona Press, 2001.

Royte, Elizabeth. *Garbage Land: On the Secret Trail of Trash.* New York: Little, Brown and Company, 2005.

U.S. Environmental Protection Agency National Priorities List, Active Superfund Sites, http://oaspub.epa.gov/superfund/sites/npl/index.htm.

Wilcox, Charlotte. *Trash!* Minneapolis: Lerner Publishing Company, 1988.

FURTHER READING

Adventures of the Garbage Gremlin
http://www.epa.gov/epaoswer/non-hw/recycle/gremlin/gremlin.htm
This comic book from the Environmental Protection Agency offers a fun and useful way to learn about trash.

Burns, Loree Griffin. *Tracking Trash: Flotsam, Jetsam, and the Science of Ocean Motion.* Boston: Houghton Mifflin, 2007. Follow Dr. Curtis Ebbesmeyer as he tracks and studies the trash that ends up in the world's oceans.

Clean Sweep U.S.A.
>http://www.cleansweepusa.org
>Find out about litter prevention, discover how recycling works, and read about
>how people can get energy from garbage.

Earth 911
>http://www.earth911.org
>Earth 911 offers hundreds of pages of information. Solid waste, recycling,
>e-cycling, and composting are a few of the topics covered on this site. The kids'
>section includes activities, games, songs, contests, and links.

Earth Works Group, The. *50 Simple Things Kids Can Do to Save the Earth.* Kansas City,
>Mo.: Andrews and McMeel, 1990. Learn all about what you can do to preserve and
>protect planet Earth.

Energy Kid's Page
>http://www.eia.doe.gov/kids
>This site from the U.S. Department of Energy includes interesting pages for kids.
>The "Energy Facts/Saving Energy" section features information on waste-to-
>energy plants and recycling.

Johnson, Rebecca L. *Understanding Global Warming.* Minneapolis: Lerner Publications
>Company, 2009. Learn all about global warming and how it affects our planet in
>this interesting selection.

Planet Protectors Club for Kids
>http://www.epa.gov/epaoswer/osw/kids
>This Environmental Protection Agency Web page contains links to games and
>activities to help kids learn about reducing wastes and saving resources.

Recyclezone
>http://www.recyclezone.org.uk/home.aspx
>Visit Recyclezone to learn all about reducing, reusing, and recycling.

Wilcox, Charlotte. *Recycling.* Minneapolis: Lerner Publishing Company, 2008. This book
>focuses on new and unique ways of recycling trash.

INDEX

71

ABOUT THE AUTHOR

Charlotte Wilcox began writing about science topics for young readers in 1988 with her first book, *Trash!* Since then she has written more than forty books for young readers, including the award-winning *Mummies and Their Mysteries* (1993) and *Mummies, Bones, and Body Parts* (2000). She continues to write about topics of environmental and social concern. In addition, she is the editor of two regional magazines in Minnesota.

PHOTO ACKNOWLEDGMENTS

The images in this book are used with the permission of: © Todd Strand/Independent Picture Service, pp. 1, 3 (top), 18 (bottom), 41, 46, 47, 61; © John Terrence Turner/drr.net, p. 3 (center); © Philip and Karen Smith/Iconica/Getty Images, p. 3 (bottom); © Jeff Breedlove/Dreamstime.com, p. 4 (foreground); NASA, p. 4 (background); © iStockphoto.com/Ever, p. 6; © VisionsofAmerica/Joe Sohm/Getty Images, p. 7 (background); © Ashley Cooper/CORBIS, p. 7 (inset); UPPA/Photoshot, p. 9; ©Ann Ronan Picture Library/Heritage-Images/The Image Works, p. 10; Mid-Manhatten Library/Picture Collection, The New York Public Library, Astor, Lenox and Tilden Foundations, p. 11; Wisconsin Historical Society (46176), p. 12; Library of Congress (LC-DIG-nclc-04803), p. 13; © Digitalfood/Dreamstime.com, p. 14; © Kevin Enns-Rempel, p. 15; © ClassicStock/Alamy, p. 16; AP Photo/David Bookstaver, p. 17; © Beth Davidow/Visuals Unlimited, p. 18 (top); © Valarie Hulstad/Independent Picture Service, p. 19 (top); © The Image Works Archive, p. 19 (bottom); © Inga Spence/Visuals Unlimited, pp. 22, 23; © Mike Norton/Dreamstime.com, p. 23 (top); ©Ray Pfortner/Peter Arnold, Inc., p. 25; © Arthur S. Aubry/Photodisc/Getty Images, p. 26; © Icefront/Dreamstime.com, p. 27; © Don Hammond/design pics/drr.net, pp. 28, 31; © Julie Caruso/Independent Picture Service, p. 29; © Peter Macdiarmid/Getty Images, p. 33; © David R. Frazier Photography/Alamy, pp. 34, 53 (inset); © felixcasio/Dreamstime.com, p. 35; © Blair M. Seitz/drr.net, p. 36; © Broker/Dreamstime.com, p. 37; ©Joe Raedle/Getty Images, p. 38; © Louie Psihoyos/Science Faction/Getty Images, p. 39; © Lee Snider/The Image Works, p. 42; © Mira/Alamy, p. 43; © Owen Brewer/ZUMA Press, p. 45; © Mark Douet/Photographer's Choice/Getty Images, p. 49 (left); © Steve Hamilton/Dorling Kindersley/Getty Images, p. 49 (right); © Jim West/The Image Works, p. 50; © Luminis/Dreamstime.com, p. 51; © Andrea Jones/Alamy, p. 53 (background); © Peter Cox/Alamy, p. 54; © Gabe Palmer/Alamy, p. 55; © Noel Hendrickson/Digital Vision/Getty Images, p. 56; AP Photo/Mark Stehle, p. 57; AP Photo/Jim Mone, p. 58; © Maximilian Stock, LTD/PHOTOTAKE, Inc./Alamy, p. 59; AP Photo/Bill Haber, p. 60; © Julie Caruso, p. 63; illustrations by Bill Hauser/Independent Picture Service.

Front cover: © Rob Walls/Alamy (top left); © iStockphoto.com/Marcus Clackson (top right); © Todd Strand/Independent Picture Service (bottom Left); © iStockphoto.com/Stephanie DeLay (background).